# Smart Contracts Unleashed

## Reinventing the Legal Landscape with Blockchain

# Table of Contents

# Chapter 1. Introduction

In this exclusive Special Report titled "Smart Contracts Unleashed: Reinventing the Legal Landscape with Blockchain", we delve into the transformative power of smart contracts powered by blockchain technology. Bridging the divide between complex legal procedures and cutting-edge technology, this report offers a refreshingly accessible explanation of how these decentralized, self-executing contracts are poised to revolutionize legal interactions and transactions. Trading jargon for simple language, we connect the dots between digital tech and real-world applications. With insightful case studies, expert opinions, and forward-thinking projections, this report is your ticket to understanding, and potentially capitalizing on, this groundbreaking shift. From seasoned attorneys to tech enthusiasts, there is something in this report for everyone: Unravel the exciting new prospects brought about by smart contracts, and why they are redefining not just the legal, but the commercial and social landscape as well. Grab your copy today!

# Chapter 2. Unveiling Blockchain and Smart Contracts: An Introduction

Blockchain technology, initially developed as the financial mechanism for the cryptocurrency Bitcoin, has spawned a multitude of new applications. Among the most promising is the advent of smart contracts. Just as traditional contracts have forever served as legally binding agreements between parties, smart contracts promise to take the efficiency and security of those agreements to unparalleled new heights.

## 2.1. The Foundational Blockchain

The foundation of it all is Blockchain, essentially a decentralized ledger or database, transparently shared across a network of computers, or nodes. Each blockchain consists of multiple blocks of data, chained together via complex mathematical algorithms. Whenever a new transaction occurs, it is recorded and added to the chain in its own block. This data is then distributed to each node in the network, and due to its cryptographic nature, it cannot be altered or deleted without consensus among the network participants.

In contrast to traditional databases, each participant has a copy of the full blockchain, creating a high degree of transparency. Furthermore, every block includes the hash of its preceding block, ensuring that any alteration of a block's content will break the chain's continuity and be recognized immediately. Such characteristics and the absence of a centralized authority make blockchains secure and particularly resistant to fraudulent activities and cyber-attacks.

## 2.2. Nature of Contracts: Evolution towards Smart Contracts

Contracts, since their inception, have been serving as facilitators of order and trust between parties. But they come with their own sets of limitations – from tedious paperwork to lengthy litigations. It is in this context that smart contracts step in. They can perform the functions traditionally carried out by legal contracts without human intervention and with a significantly higher execution speed, thanks to the code embedded in them. In essence, they are programs running on the blockchain that execute automatically when certain conditions in the agreement are met.

Nick Szabo, who coined the term "Smart Contracts" in the 1990s, defined them as computerized transaction protocols that facilitate, verify, or enforce the terms of an agreement. They were heralded as digital vending machines where users could input data or value, and receive a finite item from a machine. In many ways, smart contracts are autonomous digital agents within the blockchain ecosystem.

## 2.3. Operation of Smart Contracts

The operations of smart contracts follow the principle of the conditional "IF-THEN" statement. For instance, consider a property rental scenario in the blockchain realm. A renter wants to access a rental unit they've paid for. The smart contract ties a digital key to the payment and the agreement conditions: IF the renter pays the agreed amount on time, THEN the digital key will be released to the renter, who can then access the property. No third-party intermediaries are needed, including no property brokers, no banks, and no legal advisors.

## 2.4. Advantages and Challenges

Smart contracts proffer ample advantages. As they are automated, the execution is nearly instantaneous and transparent. These contracts are cost-effective as they remove the need for intermediaries or manual enforcement, which also significantly reduces chances of error. Their decentralized nature ensures that no single party has control, offering greater protection against fraud.

However, smart contracts have their share of challenges too. The current legal framework around the globe might find it challenging to recognize or enforce them. Due to their immutable quality, changes cannot be made once the contract is on blockchain, which can be an issue if alterations are required. There's also the risk of coding errors and security vulnerabilities that could have serious repercussions.

## 2.5. Case Study: Ethereum Platform

One of the most important players in the development of smart contracts is the Ethereum platform. Ethereum enhances the simplicity and limited functionality of Bitcoin's blockchain by offering a blockchain with a built-in fully-fledged Turing-complete programming language. This allows developers to create whatever operation they want, which can trigger complex actions when specific conditions are met.

Ethereum's smart contracts have been used for an array of applications, from creating digital marketplaces and decentralized autonomous organizations to launching initial coin offerings.

## 2.6. Conclusion: Future Prospects

The smart contract technology could impact sectors far beyond the law, with potential for broad social and commercial applications.

They could revolutionize supply chain management, enable truly peer-to-peer sharing economies, and automate insurance compensations. It's a brave new world yet to be uncovered, unbound by the scope and limits of the traditional contractual framework.

However, for smart contracts to become universally accepted and widely used, several legal and regulatory uncertainties need to be addressed. From defining legal jurisdictions to addressing instances of fraud, disputes, and errors, there is a lot of ground to cover before we mainstream smart contracts. But with the pace at which this technology is evolving, the horizon certainly looks promising.

Smart contracts embody the true disruptive potential of blockchain technology. They are poised to redefine not just the legal landscape, but the commercial and social sphere as well - making contract execution smoother, more reliable, and more efficient. The future of complexity simplified is not far off, and smart contracts are leading the way.

# Chapter 3. The Anatomy of Smart Contracts

At the heart of the technological revolution we're witnessing today is a component dubbed the "smart contract." It's not a paper document signed in ink but a digital agreement run by automated code. Just what is this technology, and how does it function? Let's dissect it to understand.

## 3.1. Blockchain: The underlying infrastructure

Smart contracts run on a technology platform named blockchain, which is, essentially, a digital ledger book, a database where transactions are recorded, and once entered, cannot be altered or deleted. Thus, by their nature, blockchains carry intrinsic value: Trustability.

Blockchain provides transparency, immutability (meaning nobody can change the content), and disintermediation (eliminating intermediaries or middlemen). This combination of attributes makes blockchain an ideal platform for smart contracts.

## 3.2. Traditional Contracts vs. Smart Contracts

To comprehend the dimension of the shift that smart contracts represent, it's essential to start by recapping the nature of a traditional contract. A standard contract is a legally binding agreement between two or more parties. The contract stipulates obligations that each party must fulfill to their mutual satisfaction. If a dispute arises, the aggrieved party can appeal to the judicial system for resolution.

Comparatively, a smart contract encodes these obligations as automatic functions executed by a computer program. This means that when certain conditions are met, the program self-activates to carry out the functions specified. It doesn't require human intervention. This leap from manual processing to automated execution represents a quantum shift in how contracts can be made and enforced.

## 3.3. Structure of a Smart Contract

Smart contracts consist of the following components:

- **Parties**: These are the entities involved in the agreement. In the digital realm, they can be people, programs, or devices.

- **Subject Matter**: This is the object or purpose of the contract. In a blockchain context, this could be a real-world asset represented digitally (a tokenized asset), or a purely digital entity like cryptocurrency.

- **Terms**: These outline the rights and obligations of the parties. In a smart contract, these are encoded as executable functions.

- **Conditions**: These are the circumstances under which the contract executes. They're formed based on 'if-this-then-that' (IFTTT) logic. When a certain condition is fulfilled (the 'if this' part), the contract executes automatically (the 'then that' part).

## 3.4. The Life Cycle of a Smart Contract

Smart contracts pass through a series of stages:

1. **Authoring**: A coder writes the contract in a programming

language like Solidity (used by Ethereum). They encode the conditions and obligations as functions.

2. **Deployment**: The contract is loaded onto the blockchain where it resides as a piece of code waiting for activation.

3. **Activation**: The contract gets activated when a transaction triggers it.

4. **Execution**: Once the required conditions are fulfilled, the contract self-executes. This can involve transferring tokens from one party to another, adjusting entries in a register, triggering other contracts, or myriad other possibilities.

## 3.5. Smart Contracts Interactions and Composability

A critical attribute of smart contracts is their ability to interact with other contracts. A smart contract can call upon other contracts, enabling complex chains of automatic actions. Not only is this 'composability' a power multiplier for smart contracts, it also underpins their ability to model complex, real-world legal and business interactions.

## 3.6. Validation, Verification, and Error Handling

Given their self-executing nature, it's crucial to validate and verify these contracts before running them. Testing for bugs and potential points of failure is a prerequisite for deployment. While the lack of intermediaries is a strength, it also potentially poses risks. An improperly coded condition could lead to contractual failures or even exploitation.

# 3.7. Future of Smart Contracts

For many, the prospect of a fully automated, unalterable contract may seem either enthralling or terrifying. However, the balance tilts towards optimism due to several reasons. Smart contracts bring speed, reduce costs, and increase efficiency. They also provide enhanced transparency, empowering less tech-savvy users to participate in digital transactions with confidence.

Undoubtedly, smart contracts are set to form a significant part of our digital future. However, the practicalities of implementation, especially regarding regulation, security, and public acceptance, require careful handling. That said, there have been an increasing number of successful deployments of smart contracts, and there's a growing interest across various sectors, all of which herald a promising future.

In closing, while we stand amidst the dawn of this revolution, the real transformative power of smart contracts—and blockchain technology—will only be fully felt when these innovations become a standard part of our everyday lives.

# Chapter 4. The Genesis Story: Blockchain and Smart Contract Evolution

Decentralization, an impactful trend that has pervaded numerous sectors of the economy over the last couple of years, owes a great deal of its inception and development to an unparalleled technology - Blockchain. Blockchain's arrival can be traced back to 2008, when an anonymous entity going by the pseudonym of Satoshi Nakamoto introduced it as an underlying protocol for Bitcoin, a digital currency. Since that breakthrough moment, blockchain technology has evolved significantly, transcending the confines of cryptocurrency into several other domains—the most notable of which is arguably the realm of contracts, represented by an innovation known as smart contracts.

## 4.1. From Physical Ledgers to Digital Blocks

To fully understand the evolution of blockchain and smart contracts, a review of systems preceding their emergence is essential. Before the digital age, financial transactions, land records, and even contracts were manually recorded in physical ledgers. This age-old practice presented a multitude of challenges, primary among which were human errors, manipulation, lack of transparency, and the potential for fraudulent activities.

The dawn of the digital epoch offered some reprieve through digital databases. Transactions, now stored in a digital ledger, seemed more reliable and efficient compared to their physical counterparts. However, these digital databases were centralized. Although they increased ease of access and reliability compared to physical ledgers, they still came with their own set of negatives including susceptibility to cyberattacks, server crashes, and still carrying potential for manipulation.

Blockchain technology came in as an innovative solution, providing a decentralized digital ledger that was transparent, secure, and almost impervious to change or deletion. Instead of one single copy stored on a local server, blockchain distributed and maintained countless copies of the database across multiple blockchain network participants - referred to as nodes. These features signaled a significant leap in the pursuit of equitable and transparent transactions in the economic world.

## 4.2. The Birth of Blockchain

Satoshi Nakamoto's seminal 2008 white paper, "Bitcoin: A Peer-to-Peer Electronic Cash System," is widely accepted as the advent of blockchain technology. Although blockchain was initially developed as an underlying component of Bitcoin to manage and record peer-to-peer transactions, its potential catalyzed its growth, extending its applications beyond cryptocurrencies. Notably, one such application that has experienced significant prominence is in facilitating contracts, bringing forth an era of Smart Contracts.

## 4.3. Enter the Age of Smart Contracts

The concept of "smart contracts" isn't exactly new. The term was first coined by Nick Szabo, a computer scientist, legal scholar and cryptographer, as early as 1994. An exemplary visionary, Szabo foresaw the potential of using a decentralized ledger to store contracts. However, the actual application of the concept had to wait for the birth of appropriate technology, which arrived with blockchain.

With blockchain technology in play, Szabo's idea suddenly became a viable reality. Smart contracts became feasible - these contracts were simple scripts or programs that automatically executed actions when predetermined conditions were met. The key feature was that these contracts self-executed, without the need for any third-party intervention or enforcement.

## 4.4. The Evolution: Smart Contracts in Real-World Applications

Moving forward from the first generation blockchain Bitcoin, newer blockchains like Ethereum provided a more versatile environment for programming smart contracts. Ethereum, introduced in 2015, broadened the horizon for use of smart contracts by incorporating a feature that enabled developers to create their own applications-including smart contracts, on its blockchain.

Smart contracts' potential applications are vast, covering domains such as finance, healthcare, real estate, and law, among others. They provide benefits like streamlined processes, reduced costs due to the absence of middlemen, increased transparency, and faster transactions. Several practical examples have emerged in recent years, from the DeFi (Decentralized Finance) movement taking the world of finance by storm with services such as lending platforms, stablecoins, and prediction markets, to real estate transactions conducted entirely through smart contracts.

## 4.5. The Story Continues: What the Future Holds

The blockchain and smart contracts evolution is far from over. Their potential to redefine legal, commercial, and even social landscapes is immense. As more sectors start recognizing and adapting the advantages of these technologies, their impacts will continue to grow. There will be regulatory and infrastructure-related challenges, but as history shows, such hurdles are not insurmountable. The pivotal point of this evolution story will remain centered around decentralization and disintermediation, bridging the gap between complex legal procedures and cutting-edge technology.

To sum up, the evolution story of blockchain and smart contracts is a continually unfolding narrative, striding steadfastly towards a future where transactions are seamless, autonomous and transparent, marking a revolutionary shift in the way we will interact and transact. From Satoshi Nakamoto to Vitalik Buterin, the journey has been unforgettable, and the destination—though not fully known—holds promising opportunities.

# Chapter 5. Smart Contracts versus Traditional Contracts

When first encountering the term "smart contract", you may wonder why the adjective "smart". Delving into this area, we discover these contracts are called so not because they hold an unrivaled understanding of law or because they have degrees from Yale. It's simply put; they are endowed with the ability to execute themselves. Once certain conditions are met, these digital contracts automatically fulfill their coded obligations, eliminating the need for intermediaries. This ability to self-execute and to self-verify its implementation makes them an intriguing advancement in contract technology.

## 5.1. The Anatomy of a Traditional Contract

A traditional contract is a formal agreement between two or more parties where legal rights and obligations are established. Ranging from house rentals to employment agreements, contracts are the cornerstone of any market economy and legal system. Traditional contracts involve tangible parameters and real-world execution, usually involving some form of "physical" interaction, e.g., someone hands you a coffee in exchange for payment.

The strength and reliability of a contract lie in the robust enforcement structure backing it, typically the legal system of a particular country. In case of a dispute, the parties can approach a court, which interprets and enforces the terms of the agreement as per the prevailing law.

## 5.2. Pain Points with Traditional Contracts

Traditional contracts, although they have stood the test of time, are not without their fair share of challenges. One of the key issues is the delay and cost involved in enforcing them. Legal fees, court delays, and administrative costs can create a significant burden.

Secondly, contracts are often challenging to understand for the layman, because they are typically written in complex and formal legal language. This complexity can sometimes lead to misunderstandings or varying interpretations.

Lastly, contracts involve a level of trust that each party involved will deliver on their promise, which always carries a risk of who will fail first. The threat of breach of contract, unfortunately, is a perennial worry in many business transactions.

## 5.3. Enter Smart Contracts

It's these perspectives and pain points that led to the conception of smart contracts. Seeded in the '90s by legal scholar and cryptographer Nick Szabo, it wasn't until the advent of blockchain technology, a decentralized digital ledger most known for powering Bitcoin, that smart contracts started to gain significant traction.

Where traditional contracts and smart contracts converge is in their intention: the agreement of terms between parties. Where they diverge is in the way in which these terms are recorded and enforced.

# 5.4. The Anatomy of a Smart Contract

A smart contract is a computer program or a transaction protocol which is intended to automatically execute, control, or document events and actions according to the terms of a contract or an agreement. It enables the action specified in the contract to happen as soon as the specified condition occurs. In other words, it's a self-operating program that automatically executes when specific conditions are met.

In a smart contract, every agreement, process, task, and payment has a digital record and a digital signature. They are stored on a blockchain, a transparent, distributed ledger where everyone on the network can see the contract details.

# 5.5. Advantages of Smart Contracts

Smart contracts come with a slew of benefits that address the limitations of traditional ones. First off, they eliminate the need for trust among the parties involved since the auto-fulfillment of the contract happens only when the agreed-upon conditions are met.

Secondly, the use of smart contracts can result in significant cost and time savings because they remove the need for intermediaries and cut out much of the paperwork. They enable transactions and agreements to be carried out among disparate, anonymous parties without the need for a central authority, external enforcement mechanism, or legal system.

Moreover, due to their automated nature, smart contracts are much faster and cheaper than traditional methods. They reduce labor-intensive processes, thus enhancing productivity and efficiency.

Finally, smart contracts allow for improved traceability and security, thanks to the immutable nature of blockchain technology. Each transaction is recorded, and cannot be changed; it can only be updated by a new transaction, which is also recorded.

# 5.6. Disadvantages of Smart Contracts

While smart contracts have a lot going for them, there are drawbacks as well. The chief one is the rigidity of code. If a mistake is made in the coding process, it can be exploited and cannot be easily amended without making a new contract.

Moreover, smart contracts are still very new, and legal jurisdictions worldwide are grappling with how to manage and regulate them. The legal status and enforceability of smart contracts remain uneasy, often hovering in a grey area.

Furthermore, smart contracts are currently limited by the computational power of the blockchain where they are deployed. Complex smart contracts or those working with large data sets may encounter performance issues.

# 5.7. The Intersection and the Future

When evaluating smart contracts against traditional contracts, it's necessary to highlight the significance of both. Smart contracts look poised to revolutionize contract law and the conduct of business generally. They provide automatic fulfillment, and they cut costs, speed-up transactions, and lessen the need for trust in third parties.

However, traditional contracts are still well-entrenched, providing recourse and flexibility in ways smart contracts can't yet. For now, traditional contracts aren't going away, but their digital counterparts are inserting themselves into more and more parts of commercial life.

The future will likely be a merging of the two types. Hybrid contracts might offer legally binding contracts, represented and automated by computer code, with critical components still writable in natural language. Smart contracts mark the birth of a new era in contractual relationships, blending the lines of traditional legal interpretations with a splash of cryptography and decentralized philosophy.

Courts of law and execution of contracts may become a thing of the past as technology provides an answer to trust, efficiency, and security. Yet, it's not bleak for lawyers or the legal profession as smart contracts increasingly shift from code is law to code with law. The automation of agreements allows legal minds to innovate and create sophisticated, complex contracts, letting lawyers focus not on the redundant routine tasks but on strategic, higher-value work.

In conclusion, while smart contracts present a transformative power, they won't entirely replace traditional contracts just yet. Instead, an intersection of the two – smart contracts and traditional contracts – will redefine the legal landscape as we know it. Understanding this evolving dynamic gives us a glimpse into the future of law and transactions, a world where legal relationships and business transactions seamlessly blend human judgement and codified protocols. As fascinating as this space might be, it remains in its nascence and carries accordingly the potential of a digital contract frontier, prepared for further exploration and increased utilization.

# Chapter 6. Applications of Smart Contracts in the Legal Realm

Smart contracts, the backbone of many blockchain platforms, have the potential to create radical changes in the legal realm. Their potential for automating and enforcing legal commitments makes them an ideal tool for a wide range of legal applications.

## 6.1. The Basics of Smart Contracts

To understand how smart contracts impact the legal realm, it is vital to comprehend what they are. Smart contracts are computer programs that facilitate, verify, or enforce the performance or negotiation of a contract. They run on blockchain technology, a distributed ledger that records transactions across many computers in such a way that the involved records cannot be altered retroactively.

Smart contracts are called "smart" because they automatically execute when predefined conditions are met. No intermediaries are needed to monitor compliance or facilitate execution. They are tamper-proof, transparent, and as immutable as the blockchains they reside on.

Moreover, smart contracts present an opportunity for legal professionals to automate a large part of their work, increase efficiency, and reduce the legal uncertainty that often comes with traditional contract law.

## 6.2. Smart Contracts Vs Traditional Contracts

Before delving into applications, it's beneficial to differentiate between traditional contracts and smart ones. Both serve to enforce agreement between parties. However, where traditional contracts necessitate a trusted third party—be it a courtroom, lawyer, or notary—smart contracts leverage the immutability and distributed nature of blockchain to eliminate the need for such an intermediary.

A significant downside to traditional contracts is the ambiguity in language and interpretation that often leads to contractual disputes. Smart contracts, being machine readable, demand precise and unambiguous language which reduces the potential for disputes.

## 6.3. Use Cases within the Legal Industry

Within the legal realm, various sectors could be disrupted and enhanced by smart contracts.

1. Property ownership and real estate: Property transfer typically involves various parties and copious paperwork. Smart contracts could simplify this procedure by automating it. Once conditions of sale are satisfied like payment and document verification, the property's ownership is automatically transferred to the buyer. This reduces the need for third-party involvement and lowers the associated costs and time.

2. Intellectual Property: Smart contracts could be harnessed to protect intellectual property rights, govern licensing agreements, and facilitate royalty payments. For instance, a smart contract on a song could ensure that every time the song is played, a defined percentage of royalty is automatically transferred to the song's

rights holder.

3. Wills and inheritance: By using smart contracts, the distribution of assets after a person's death can be greatly simplified. The contract could be programmed to automatically divide assets between heirs as per the deceased person's wishes, reducing bureaucracy and potential family conflicts.

4. Arbitration: Smart contracts could be dominantly used in dispute resolution. They offer transparency in the arbitration process and can be programmed to release funds or enforce penalties once arbitral decisions have been reached.

# 6.4. Limitations and Legal Considerations

Despite these advantages, there are limitations and legal considerations. For instance, the immutability of blockchain is a double-edged sword. Errors in the code or unforeseen circumstances may require contract modification, currently a challenging aspect of smart contracts.

Legal jurisdiction is another aspect. With parties from across the globe potentially entering into a contract, which law governs these agreements? This, alongside the anonymity that often comes with blockchain transactions, poses significant challenges to legal enforcement.

Smart contracts also don't entirely eliminate the need for lawyers. Legal advice is crucial to ensure that the smart contract's code properly reflects the parties' intentions and complies with relevant laws and regulations.

# 6.5. The Future of Smart Contracts in Law

In the future, we can expect further evolution and specialization of smart contracts in the legal industry. Their potential to improve efficiency, reduce disputes, and streamline processes is substantial. As the technology matured and the industry gains more understanding, we can expect to see smart contracts being widely adopted across many legal operations.

Meanwhile, the legal landscape will have to evolve as well to vest smart contracts with cryptographically secured legal weight. The development of an appropriate regulatory and legal framework that governs smart contracts is a necessary condition for this transformation.

# 6.6. Concluding Remarks

Smart contracts have the potential to create deep ripples in the legal landscape. As the technology matures, they will revolutionise the way we think about and use contracts. The digitization of contracts through smart contracts provides a unique intersection of law and technology, paving the way for an exciting new era for the legal profession. The legal sector must adapt and grow in alignment with these Digital Age advancements to fully capitalize on their benefits and meet the future's challenges. As we stand on the cusp of this technological revolution, the legal realm braced for transformation is an absolute certainty. The question is not if, but when and to what extent.

# Chapter 7. Demystifying the Technology behind Smart Contracts

Understanding a smart contract requires first engaging with the technology behind it. Simplified at its core, it is a fusion of legal contract theory and computer programming, imbued with the hallmarks of blockchain technology – decentralization, immutability, and security.

## 7.1. The Concept of Blockchain

To comprehend smart contracts, one must grasp the underlying blockchain technology. Imagine a digital ledger, a vast spreadsheet, duplicated across a network of computers (nodes) running this ledger on a peer-to-peer (P2P) basis using a secure, time-stamped mechanism. It's a database management system in a sense, where digital information can be recorded and shared, but from which existing data cannot be retroactively altered without the consensus of the network and then altering all subsequent blocks.

The blockchain carries a series of blocks, each holding a list of transactions. Every transaction is encoded into a 'hash' at the block's inception – a complex algorithm producing a unique code, which is impacted by even the smallest modification of the data it represents. Creating a new block involves the system threading a hash back to the previous block, forming a chain of blocks – a blockchain.

Thus, blockchains are robust; hack one block, and the entire chain breaks, signaling an anomaly. Changes in one block requires adjustments in all blocks, needing the majority of the network's consent – a feature delivering an unprecedented level of security and trust.

# 7.2. The Power of Decentralization

Decentralization is one of the key defining features of blockchain. Conventional systems rely on a central authority—banks for financial transactions, or government bodies for records. These intermediaries verify, record, and coordinate all transactions. Blockchain, however, eschews any central authority. All participating nodes have access to the whole ledger, and consensus, rather than a central authority, drives validation.

This decentralization results in a system that is transparent and highly resistant to censorship. It reduces the potential points of vulnerability that hackers can exploit and hence the chances of fraudulent activity. The peer-to-peer system also accelerates processes as there is no need for validation from a centralized authority.

# 7.3. The Essence of Smart Contracts

With the understanding of blockchain technology is in place, we turn to smart contracts. The idea was first proposed back in 1994 by Nick Szabo, a cryptographer and computer scientist. He envisioned contracts upgraded with software, enabling them to execute when the agreed terms are met automatically. Smart contracts, according to him, are computerized transaction protocols that execute the terms of a contract.

Smart contracts are not simply contracts transcribed into code; they possess the capabilities to execute themselves upon meeting set conditions. Encoded as a set of rules on the blockchain, they automatically ensure the obligations of a contract are carried out, without human intervention.

# 7.4. Anatomy of a Smart Contract

In more concrete terms, smart contracts are computer programs running on top of a blockchain. Following a specific programming language, like Solidity for Ethereum, they include clauses outlined by the creators, which, in turn, trigger specific actions when pre-set conditions are met.

For instance, consider a rental agreement as a smart contract. The tenant pays the digital currency into the smart contract—the landlord does not receive it yet. On the agreed move-in day, the smart contract checks if the payment is made. If so, it releases an encrypted digital key to the tenant to access the home. If not, the smart contract automatically refunds the tenant.

This procedure exhibits why trustworthiness is inherent in smart contracts. The contract self-executes, and only then does the agreed exchange occur, minimizing uncertainties or fraudulent practices.

# 7.5. The Life-cycle of a Smart Contract

Smart contracts go through various stages from creation to execution. Initialization involves the contract's deployment on the blockchain, which includes coding the contract conditions. Following deployment, the contract's immutable—no modifications can be made to the agreed terms. Once the conditions for execution are met, the contract automatically executes itself. Finally, after executing all conditions, it ends.

# 7.6. Benefits, Limitations, and Potential Solutions

Smart contracts offer various benefits, such as cost-effectiveness, efficiency, and trust. They eliminate the need for intermediaries in transactions, saving costs, time, and effort. The contracts' automatic, transparent nature makes them a trusted solution for business interactions, mitigating risks of manipulation, fraud, and error.

But the benefits come with limitations. Most notably is the challenge of coding legal agreements accurately and foreseeably to account for all possible contingencies. Smart contracts' immutable nature, while a security boon, also means once deployed, coding errors are also incapable of alteration. This limitation is a pressing issue in today's fast-paced, evolving digital world.

With time, solutions like 'upgradable contracts' and 'off-chain computations' are being developed to deal with these issues, but they need more testing and development. Hence, while heralding a promising era of secure, quick, and automatic enforcing of agreements, smart contracts need to evolve to address current challenges perfectly.

Barely scratching the potential of this technology, smart contracts offer a world of possibilities. As the wrinkles iron out over time, we stand on the precipice of a revolution, where blockchain and smart contracts could redefine our understanding of contractual law and business dealings.

# Chapter 8. Disruption in the Legal Landscape: Case Studies

In the rapidly evolving digital world, legal processes are being disrupted by smart contracts. Traditional legal documents are a conduit marked by long turnover times, high costs, and opportunities for fraudulence—issues that blockchain and the smart contracts it enables are well positioned to tackle.

## 8.1. The Basics of Smart Contracts

Smart contracts are self-executing contracts with the terms of the agreement directly written into lines of code. The code not only contains the rules and penalties around the agreement, but also the mechanisms to enforce them. They operate on the blockchain network—a decentralized and distributed digital ledger that records transactions across many computers, ensuring data transparency and security.

A written contract needs third parties for verification and enforcement. However, smart contracts automate execution by using code to implement contractual obligations. Once a smart contract's conditions are met, actions are automatically triggered, eliminating the need for intermediaries.

## 8.2. Unleashing Efficiency on Real Estate Transactions

Consider the case of real estate transactions typically chained to lengthy chains of processes—property search, negotiations, bank financing, due diligence, and contract signing. Smart contracts can revolutionize this process. Once the buyer and seller agree to terms, they can be encoded in a smart contract. When the buyer transfers the agreed amount to the smart contract, ownership rights are transferred automatically, eliminating middlemen, and making the process faster and error-free.

## 8.3. Restructuring Intellectual Property Rights

Blockchain's immutable ledger combined with smart contracts can address challenges in intellectual property rights ownership. Artists and creators can register their work on blockchain, creating a tamper-proof record. When someone wants to use a creative piece, the process—from agreement, payment to content delivery—can be handled by a smart contract, ensuring the artist is fairly compensated.

## 8.4. Transforming Supply Chain Operations

The supply chain landscape, replete with opacity, offline documentation, and fraudulent behaviours, stands to gain from smart contract implementation. A smart contract can track production, packaging, and delivery, automatically releasing payments upon verification of each step. This increases operational efficiency, reduces fraud, and improves tracking, bringing unmatched transparency.

## 8.5. Reshaping Insurance Claims

Claim processes in insurance is another area where smart contracts can disrupt the status quo. Smart contracts can automatically verify claims and trigger payments, cutting down lengthy claim verification processes. This not only expedites the claim process but also reduces opportunities for fraud.

# 8.6. The Hurdles Ahead

Despite the potential, several barriers to the widespread adoption of smart contracts remain. Regulatory uncertainty, lack of legal recognition, contract ambiguity, and technological constraints are significant stumbling blocks. For smart contracts to function effectively, laws must acknowledge and enforce them—however, many jurisdictions are yet to provide clear guidelines. Technologically, issues like code bugs and scalability can impact the effectiveness of smart contracts.

# 8.7. Conclusion: Towards a Smart Legal Landscape

A tech-driven legal landscape seems inevitable, with smart contracts leading the way. By offering speed, efficiency, transparency, and security, they promise to transform traditional legal processes. While challenges lie ahead, as technology evolves and legal frameworks adapt, smart contracts will likely disrupt the legal landscape in ways we can barely imagine today. However, for a smooth transition, an understanding of this innovative technology is essential.

This report has aimed to illuminate the concept, potential, and challenges of smart contracts with insights from experts and real-world case studies. The expanding realm of blockchain technology reaches across various industries. As we look ahead, the impact of smart contracts on the legal and commercial landscape appears immense and largely momentous.

# Chapter 9. The Road Ahead: Predictive Analysis for Smart Contracts

In the ever-evolving world of blockchain and digitized contracts, few technologies have been quite as transformative or have demonstrated as much potential as smart contracts. As their use expands, it is essential to look ahead and analyze the likely trajectories of this budding sector.

## 9.1. The Growing Importance of Smart Contracts

The efficacy of any digital transaction is predicated on the security of the exchange, and the assurance of agreement fulfillment. Traditionally, these elements have been enforced by legal procedures - yet as our world grows increasingly digital, these protocols often prove inflexible or inefficient. Smart contracts provide a promising solution to these problems.

Analogous to traditional contracts, smart contracts are determined by strict rules and conditions, but dispense with the need for intermediaries. Using blockchain technology, these contracts are self-verifying, self-executing, and resistant to modification. In a sense, they represent a fusion of law, economics, and computer science, promising to automate, simplify, and secure a vast array of transactions.

Across industries, an increasing number of businesses and organizations are recognizing the benefits of incorporating smart contracts into their operations. Industries such as supply chain, real estate, healthcare, and finance, among others, are already adopting these digitized contract systems. The reason is simple: smart contracts offer a streamlined, trustworthy, and cost-effective method for carrying out transactions.

## 9.2. Prospective Developments: From Transactional to Transformational

As we move forward, smart contracts are expected to transition from being a transactional tool to a transformational one. The future will likely see smart contracts integrated with other nascent technologies such as IoT and AI to create groundbreaking systems that can self-manage, self-diagnose, and self-fix, offering unprecedented levels of operational efficiency.

Envision a future where smart cities are powered by interconnected systems of smart contracts, IoT devices, and AI protocols. Traffic lights communicate with each other to manage traffic flows, supply chains self-organize based on demand signals, energy grids intelligently allocate resources - the possibilities are immense and inspiring.

## 9.3. Risks and Challenges

In spite of the extraordinary potential of smart contracts, their journey is not without obstacles. Understanding these challenges is integral to facilitating mainstream adoption and encouraging further innovation.

One critical challenge that smart contracts face is the issue of legality. As of now, the legal standing of smart contracts is still ambiguous. Given that they automatically execute predefined programming instructions, there are concerns about what happens when disputes arise. This challenge reiterates the need for continued dialogue between technologists, legislators, and legal practitioners to ensure that future laws accommodate and regulate the use of smart contracts.

Cybersecurity is another hurdle that smart contracts must overcome. Since these contracts are self-executing and immutable, they are potentially attractive targets for cybercriminals. Overcoming this hurdle will require advancements in cybersecurity, contract programming practices, and perhaps even our understanding of trust in the digital realm.

## 9.4. The Key to Unlocking the Potential: Interoperability

For smart contracts to become commonplace and realize their full potential, interoperability will be paramount. In essence, different smart contract networks should be able to communicate and operate with each other. Blockchain is a multi-network ecosystem, and lack of interoperability could lead to the problem of isolated network silos, limiting the true power of these technologies.

Currently, different blockchain protocols which smart contracts ride on have different programming languages, consensus mechanisms, and business models which makes them incompatible with each other. Therefore, fostering interoperability calls for creating a unified framework or standards for different blockchain technologies to interact and communicate. The introduction of blockchain bridges is one solution that developers are exploring to mitigate this.

## 9.5. Conclusion

In conclusion, the world of smart contracts is evolving fast, and there is much to anticipate. As more businesses start to comprehend the effectiveness of these mechanisms, we stand on the verge of seeing a mass adoption of this technology across industries. The challenges are present, but they represent an opportunity for growth and creativity in our journey towards a decentralized future. Whether one is a technophile or a casual observer, it's undeniable - smart contracts are poised to revolutionize our world, and these are exciting times for everyone involved.

# Chapter 10. Overcoming the Challenges: Law and Order in the Blockchain Era

While blockchain technology, with its promise of transparency, decentralization, and security, presents an array of lucrative opportunities, its successful implementation is not without roadblocks, particularly within the legal framework. This chapter seeks to elucidate the significant challenges associated with the meeting point of law and blockchain, and offers solutions for a smooth, compliant, and effective integration of this groundbreaking technology into our legal reality.

## 10.1. Regulation – The Elephant in the Room

Regulation represents perhaps the largest hurdle in the acceptance and integration of blockchain into our legal infrastructure. Blockchain, in design and function, is borderless, making its regulation a monumental task. Policymakers struggle to devise a universally acceptable framework due to vastly different local regulations and jurisdictional issues.

The lack of a unanimous regulatory framework subjects blockchain applications, such as cryptocurrencies and smart contracts, to scrutiny and distrust. This has significant implications for its mass adoption. Regulatory clarity will permit organizations to make sustained investments in the technology, secure in their compliance with law.

The necessity for regulation extends beyond legal compliance; it also addresses concerns surrounding privacy, tax, and crime prevention.

The distribution of ownership data, and even personal identification data, over a broad network can result in serious privacy concerns. Cryptocurrency has been used for tax evasion and illicit activities, owing to its anonymity. A solid legal structure can address these caveats, thus legitimizing and enhancing the image of blockchain.

## 10.2. Legal Enforceability of Blockchain Transactions

Smart contracts, though programmatically precise, are embryonic in the eyes of the law. Primarily, there is a question of enforceability. Smart contracts stack digital agreements into blocks, which are then attached to the chain rendering them 'immutable'. But what happens when contractual errors are involved, or when contracts need to be invalidated?

Some argue that traditional legal frameworks can be expanded to include smart contracts – similar to how electronic signatures were eventually classified with their ink counterparts. To succeed, enforcers, such as courts and arbitration entities, need to understand and accept the validity of blockchain transactions. This gives rise to the question of whether legal professionals are equipped with the necessary knowledge and adaptability to accommodate the language of code.

## 10.3. Reconciling Central Authority with Decentralization

Blockchain and legal systems are at odds with regard to central authority. On one hand, the legal system thrives on centralized authority in enforcing law and order, while blockchain is built on the foundation of decentralization – removing the need for middlemen and enabling peer-to-peer transactions. This discrepancy raises questions on how disputes are to be resolved and fraudulent activities tackled.

# 10.4. Toward a Blockchain-Compatible Legal System

Given the vast complexities surrounding blockchain and the law, it's essential to pave the way for their seamless cohabitation. Firstly, a concerted effort must be made to educate those within the legal profession about blockchain technology. This will not only facilitate the drafting of blockchain-suitable laws, but also ensure their just enforcement.

Secondly, creating blockchain sandboxes might provide a safe space for innovators to test their blockchain applications against real-world scenarios without fear of persecution. This can lead the way in understanding the system's vulnerabilities and is integral for drafting effective legislation.

Lastly, the implementation of blockchain into governance can play a pivotal role in demonstrating the technology's capabilities to the public sector. Estonia, for instance, is already using blockchain for health, judicial, legislative, security, and other systems.

Exploring and addressing these intertwined challenges can clear the path for blockchain to revolutionize our world, unleashing its vast potential across the judicial system, commerce, and societal constructs. Each step taken towards resolving these hurdles not only amplifies the transformative power of blockchain, but also brings us closer to a future where law and digitization can coexist harmoniously and effectively.

# Chapter 11. The Future in our Hands: Smart Contracts and Social Impact

At this particular juncture of digital transformation, it is not hyperbole to claim that smart contracts have the potential to significantly influence and shape our societal structures. By leveraging the capabilities of blockchain technology, these programmable instruments offer an unprecedented level of efficiency, transparency, and security. Herein, we delve thoroughly into the societal implications and potential impacts of smart contracts, assuming the vantage point of a future transformed by this groundbreaking invention.

## 11.1. Ubiquitous Presence, Seamless Transactions

In essence, smart contracts serve as self-executing contracts with the agreement written into lines of code housed in a decentralized blockchain network. As a society, we engage in contractual undertakings daily — from mundane activities like buying a cup of coffee to grand commitments like purchasing a home. Imagine, then, how our world might be revolutionized as smart contracts begin to supersede traditional contracts. A day may come when buying a house doesn't necessitate lengthy legal procedures, endless paper trails, and bureaucratic roadblocks. Instead, the transaction will be governed by a coded agreement on a public ledger, accessible by all and susceptible to tampering by none.

## 11.2. Democratizing Access and Opportunity

Smart contracts also represent a significant stride towards the democratization of opportunity. Today's society is often marked by disparities of access to resources, financial services, and opportunities reliant on one's location, economic status, or existing institutions. By contrast, smart contracts operate within a decentralized, borderless environment devoid of intermediaries. Microloans, insurance, and crowdfunds could be programmed to be accessible to anyone, anywhere, enabling opportunities to be pursued without any geographical, developmental, or bureaucratic boundaries.

## 11.3. Reinventing Governance

Smart contracts, accompanied by the blockchain's inherent transparency and security, promise to redefine the landscape of governance and enforcement, especially concerning public administration and services. Bureaucracy could transform as smart contracts automate processes, minimizing human intervention, and thus the potential for corruption or biased enforcement. Governance could become more responsive, efficient, and accountable as it pivots towards digitization.

## 11.4. Reshuffling Power Structures

As with any potentially transformative technology, there are important questions about how smart contracts might affect power and control within societies. By disintermediating transactions and interactions, smart contracts could challenge traditional power structures and enhance personal autonomy. However, where decentralized power goes, centralized power often follows. This decentralization could be counterbalanced by the rise of new power structures focused on the control of technology and data.

## 11.5. Socio-Economic Implications

Smart contracts could induce profound socio-economic changes. As transactions become seamless and efficient, traditional businesses vested in mediation and validation might find themselves obsolete. This may spur rapid economic shifts, creating new job categories while phasing out others. As a society, the effects of these changes on income distribution, employment, and workplace skills will need to be carefully managed.

## 11.6. Techno-legal Conundrums

The marriage of law and technology in smart contracts is nothing short of revolutionary but also creates its own set of complex issues. Legal frameworks worldwide still grapple with integration, recognition, and enforcement of digital contracts. The preponderance of smart contracts might necessitate a revamping of our legal systems, leading to nuances in techno-legal conundrums that societies must be ready to address.

At this point, we stand at the precipice of this interesting conceptual terrain where our existing socio-legal paradigms interact with the techno-centric ethos of smart contracts. What lies ahead is an intriguing journey requiring us to navigate precedents, broach uncharted territories, and evolve in response to the potent agency of smart contracts.

The future, as always, is in our hands; this time, coded in the language of smart contracts on the immutable fabric of a blockchain network. Today we speculate, hypothesize, and build the scaffolds. Tomorrow, we might just live in a world more fair, accessible, and efficient, one smart contract at a time.

* 9 7 9 8 8 5 6 4 9 8 6 4 5 *